Hodder & Stoughton was used to prepare the full color art.

Published by Sourcebooks eXplore an imprint of
Sourcebooks Kids
P.O. Box 4410, Naperville, Illinois 60567–4410
(630) 961-3900
sourcebookskids.com

Cataloging-in-Publication Data is on file with the Library of Congress.

Source of Production: China
Date of Production: December 2022
Run Number: 5029685
Printed and bound in China.

RRD 10 9 8 7 6 5 4 3 2 1

THIS IS OUR PLANET

A FIRST LOOK AT TAKING CARE OF NATURE

Written by
PAT THOMAS

Illustrated by
CLAIRE KEAY

sourcebooks eXplore

This is our home – and it's a special place.

It's special because, out of all the planets that we know about, it is the only one that is full of life.

Earth is the only place where there are forests, deserts and fields, mountains and valleys, oceans and rivers, birds and butterflies, elephants and earthworms ...

... and it's the only place
where there are people.

All the living things on Earth are connected because we all need to share the natural resources of the planet in order to survive.

Natural resources are things like soil, sunlight, air, oil, minerals and water, all the trees and other plants, and the animals.

Humans don't make them – nature does.

WHAT ABOUT YOU?

Can you think of some things that you have that come from nature?

Everything humans make and use comes from something made by nature.

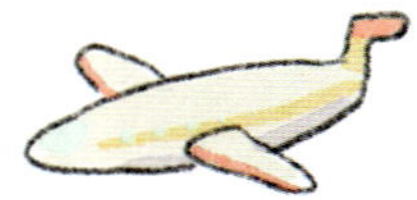

When we grow food and eat it ...

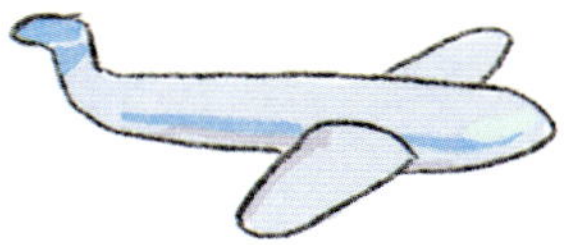

When we switch on lights, heat, TVs and computers ...

When we turn on the tap to get water ...

When we put gas in our cars and trucks ...

When we build houses, factories, shopping centers, roads and airports we are using up resources that come from nature.

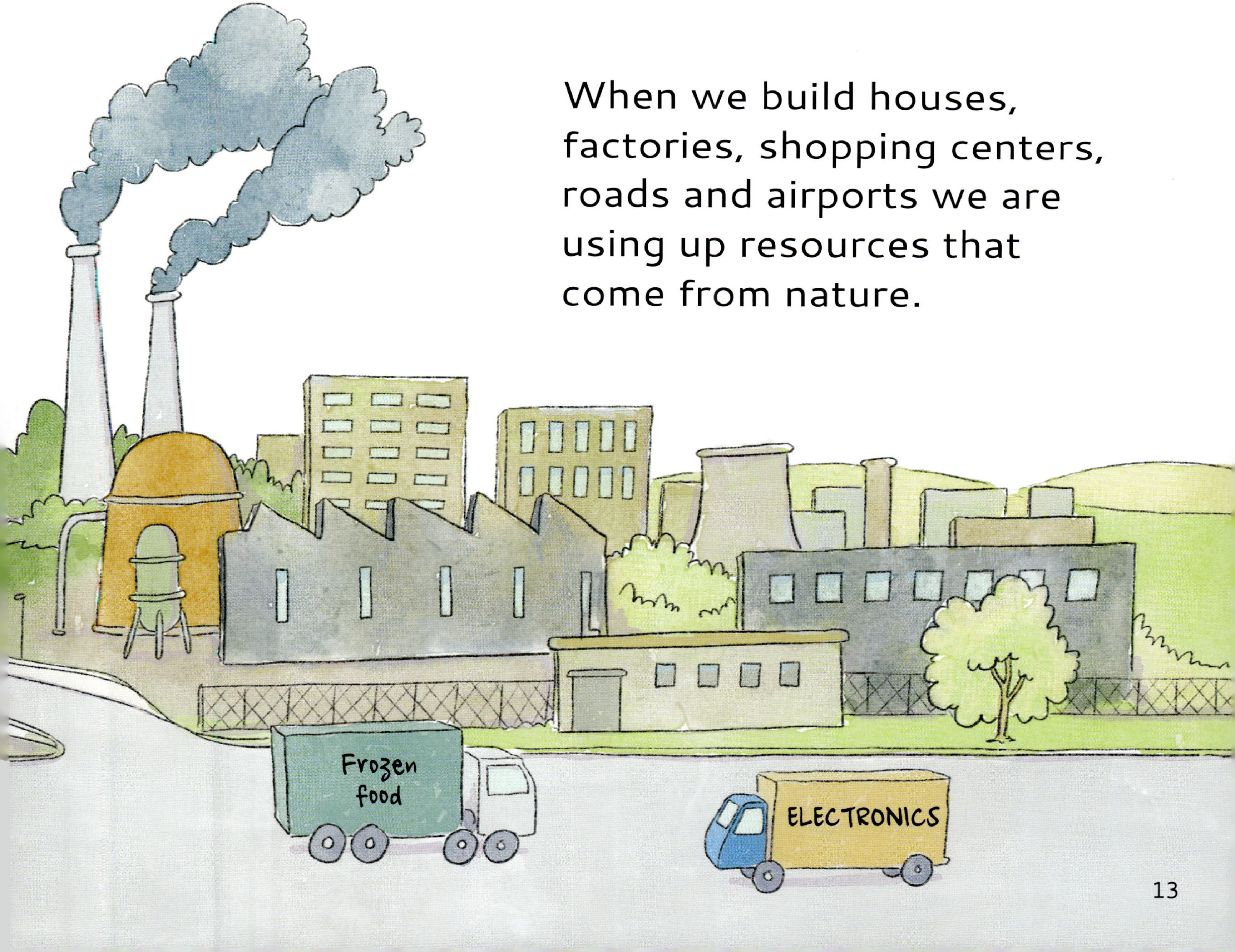

Some natural resources are renewable.

A renewable resource is one that, over time, can grow again or be made again by nature. Wood from trees, soil, sunlight, and water are renewable resources.

But some natural resources are non-renewable.

A non-renewable resource is something that cannot be replaced or would take a very long time – maybe even millions of years – for nature to make it again. Oil and coal are non-renewable resources.

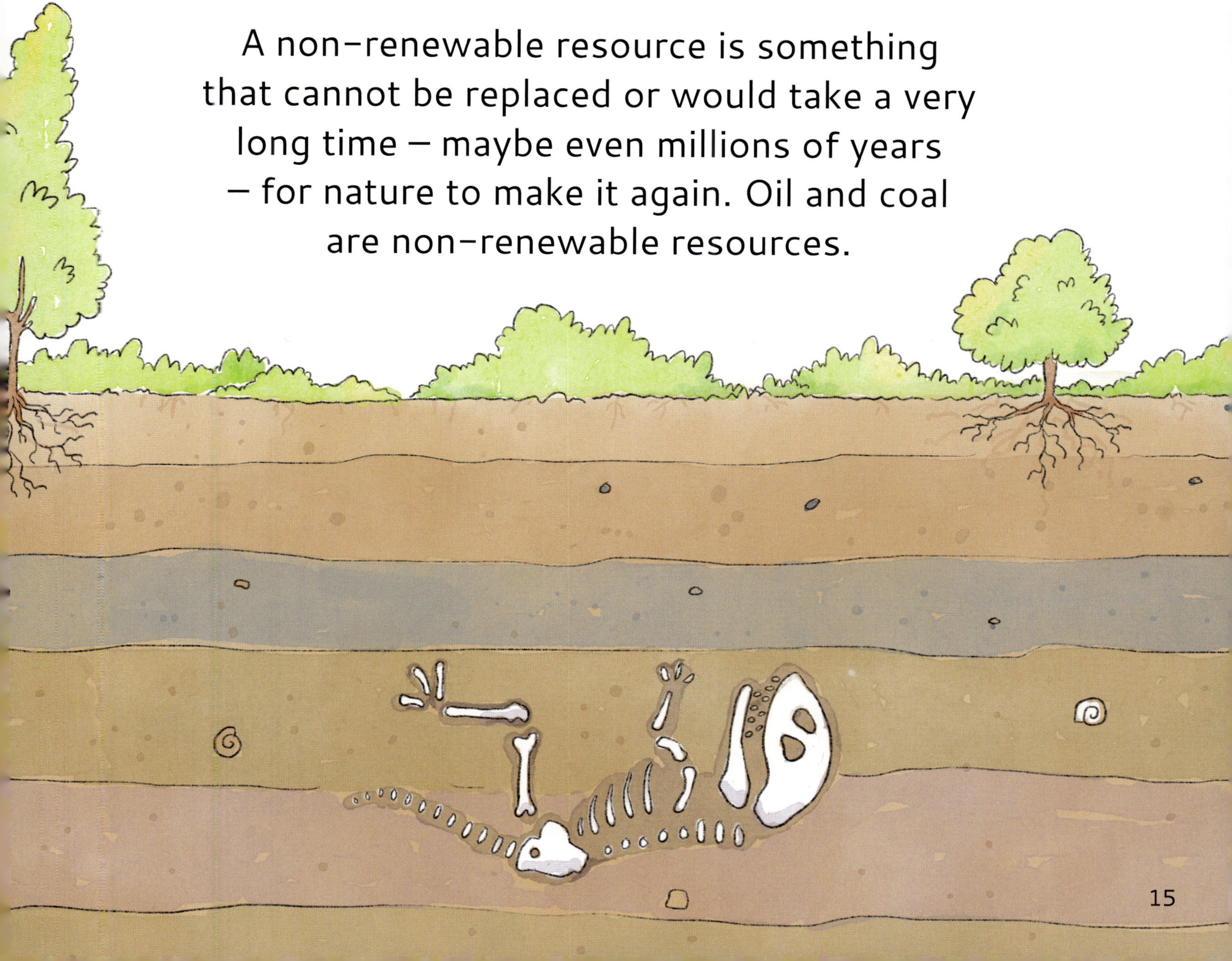

Most people understand that we need to protect and take care of the things that are special to us.

Taking care of things means they will last longer.

But right now, humans are not taking very good care of Earth.

We are using up all of nature's resources and polluting the air, water, and soil. We are cutting down trees, digging huge holes to find more coal, oil, and gas – and we are littering the planet with things we don't use any more.

Humans have also been very bad at taking care of other living creatures. By taking most of nature's resources for ourselves, we have caused many animals, insects, and plants to lose their homes, to die, and even become extinct.

Extinct means they are gone forever.

WHAT ABOUT YOU?

Can you think of some ways we are harming Earth? What things would you miss most if they disappeared forever?

We haven't always known the best way to care for the planet.

In the past, many people thought it was okay to dump poisonous chemicals into our water, to cut down forests, and let pollution from cars and factories fill the air.

But as plants and animals
and insects started disappearing
and people started to get sick,
we have learned that we
have to take better care
of Earth and ourselves.

It's not easy, but we can all learn to think differently and make better choices. All it takes is practice.

Every day we can clean up our messes.

We can turn off lights and faucets when we aren't using them.

We can reuse or fix things instead of throwing them away.

We can share what we have
and not take more than we need.

And we can work together because we get more done and feel better when we do.

WHAT ABOUT YOU?

Can you think of some things we can all do to take care of our planet?

It doesn't matter who you are or how old you are – everyone can speak out when they see someone or something that is hurting our planet.

We can ask our families, schools, and communities
to show care and respect for nature.

We can ask our governments
to make better laws to protect Earth.

We can look all around us and see what needs fixing or changing.

And even if it's hard, we can work together
to fix and change things so that now,
and in the future, all the living things
on our planet can grow and play
and live in safety and peace.

HOW TO USE THIS BOOK

Children are naturally curious about the world around them. This natural curiosity is the launchpad for helping children to develop a sense of respect and caring for the environment. In the youngest children, facts and figures may be less important than encouraging a sense of wonder and joy at being in, and exploring, the natural world around them at home, at school, and in the community.

This book is written from the perspective that we take care of the things we care about and that the rules for taking care of the environment are little different from the rules of everyday living and getting along with others. Try reading through it first and familiarizing yourself with its content before you begin.

The "What about you?" questions throughout can be useful prompts for understanding things from your child's point of view. You may find benefit in reading the book with your child more than once. Repetition allows young children to formulate thoughts and questions as the need arises.

Start small. Do something in the environment your child is familiar with and feels comfortable in. Grow a plant on the windowsill, put up a bird feeder or a windsock, turn over a rock or explore a single tree in a garden or park before venturing further afield to nature reserves and wild environments.

Be child-led. Start with what your child likes or feels drawn to. Whether it's little bugs or big cats, ponds or oceans, there are many specialist organizations that can help with child-friendly information and ideas.

Don't expect too much too soon. "The environment" is a complex topic with a long learning curve. Your child might enthusiastically embrace environmentalism only to quickly lose interest. Don't force it. Very young children can find it hard to empathize with people and situations outside of their limited frame of reference. Understanding will develop over time and often is not a straight path.

Be honest, but not alarmist. Reports of "eco-anxiety" even in very young children suggest we are still struggling to find the right balance in the conversation. Yes, the world is facing some very important environmental challenges, but young children have neither the capacity nor the agency to take responsibility for these things. Through your words and actions, aim to inspire rather than instil fear.

Encourage personal responsibility. Children follow the lead of the adults in their lives. Your enjoyment of nature, your sense of responsibility and willingness to be eco-friendly, will encourage similar sensibilities in your children. Find ways of working ecological topics into the conversation. Show respect for living things by handling plants and animals with care, put garbage in garbage cans, turn off lights and taps when not in use, get the family involved in local projects, recycle, upcycle and mend things, and explain to your child why doing these things is important to you.

...but don't let big polluters off the hook. Responsibility for environmental damage doesn't lie only with individuals. The actions of large corporations, global markets, unchecked industrialization and the impact of weak environmental regulations are hugely influential.

As the schoolchildren strikes around the world have highlighted, it is important to hold the adults who are currently running the world accountable.

Schools can help. Use every resource. Treating environmental issues strictly as STEM (science, technology, engineering and math) subjects misses the point about human engagement with nature. UNESCO acknowledges that building a sustainable world also requires qualities abundant in the arts and humanities: the power of creativity, free thinking, imagination, values, worldviews and cultural differences, and so-called "soft skills" like philosophy, self-awareness, faith, and intuition.

Take children on a fact finding mission in the community. What plants can they see, how many local trees, birds, flowers, and insects can they name? Create a mural that depicts what you find.

School gardens help children understand life cycles, seasons, ecosystems, wildlife, and caring for other living things. If the garden has edible plants in, it can be a catalyst for early discussions on where food comes from.

Engage children in discussions and projects about "eco heroes" like Jane Goodall, David Attenborough or Rachel Carson and Greta Thunberg, who have helped raise awareness of environmental causes.

Do an environmental audit of the classroom. How environmentally friendly is it? Encourage children to make suggestions and take responsibility for making the rules that make the classroom greener.

FURTHER READING

17 Ways to Save the World
by Louise Spilsbury and the United Nations
(Franklin Watts, 2020)

Be an Eco Hero series: **At Home; In Your Community; On the Move; Outdoors**
by Florence Urquhart
(Franklin Watts, 2022)

Eco Stories for those who Dare to Care
by Ben Hubbard
(Franklin Watts, 2020)

I'm Glad There Are series: **Bees and Other Bugs; Clouds and Rain; Humans and other Animals; Oceans and Seas; Stars and the Moon; Trees and Other Plants**
by Tracey Turner
(Franklin Watts, 2022)

Grandpa's Garden
by Stella Fry
(Barefoot Books, 2012)

Greta and the Giants
by Zoe Tucker
(Frances Lincoln Children's Books, 2019)

Mucky Minibeasts series: **Ants; Centipedes and Millipedes; Snails; Worms**
by Susie Williams
(Wayland, 2019)